NO
BETTER
HOPE

What **THE**
LINCOLN MEMORIAL
Means to America

BRENT ASHABRANNER

Photographs by
JENNIFER ASHABRANNER

Twenty-First Century Books
Brookfield, Connecticut

Photographs courtesy of AP/Wide World Photos: pp. 9, 10;
National Archives: pp. 17, 32, 40, 44, 47, 49, 50; Martha Ashabranner: p. 33.

Library of Congress Cataloging-in-Publication Data
Ashabranner, Brent K., 1921–
No better hope : what the Lincoln Memorial means to America/Brent Ashabranner;
photographs by Jennifer Ashabranner and historical photographs.
p. cm.–(Great American memorials)
Includes bibliographical references and index.
ISBN 0-7613-1523-3 (lib. bdg.)
1. Lincoln Memorial (Washington, D.C.)—History—Juvenile literature. 2. Lincoln, Abraham,
1809-1865—Influence—Juvenile literature. 3. Washington (D.C.)—Buildings,
structures, etc.—Juvenile literature. I Ashabranner, Jennifer, ill. II. Title.
F203.4.L73 A845 2001
975.3–dc21
00-061546

Published by Twenty-First Century Books
A Division of The Millbrook Press
2 Old New Milford Road
Brookfield, Connecticut 06804
www.millbrookpress.com

CONTENTS

Why should there not be a patient confidence
in the ultimate justice of the people?
Is there any better or equal
hope in the world?

———

Abraham Lincoln
First Inaugural Address

AUTHOR'S NOTE

My Lincoln,
My Lincoln Memorial

ALL THE BOOKS I HAVE WRITTEN—forty-two by my last count—have in some way come out of my life experiences or have been inspired by them. This book about the Lincoln Memorial is not an exception.

I discovered Abraham Lincoln when I was a boy in high school in the small Oklahoma town of Bristow. Curiously, I discovered Lincoln through poetry. I was trying to write poetry and was reading poetry both because I liked it and to help me learn to write it. One of my favorite poets was an American poet named Vachel Lindsay, and the poem of his that I liked best was called "Abraham Lincoln Walks at Midnight." It is about the ghost of Lincoln walking at night in Springfield, Illinois, where he is buried, and feeling the pain of World War I.

Another poet I read was Edwin Markham. His most famous poem was "The Man with the Hoe," but my favorite of his poems was "Lincoln, the Man of the People." Markham called Lincoln "a man to match the mountains and the sea" and compared him to a great tree in a forest. When it falls, it leaves "a lonesome place against the sky." I was also especially drawn to Walt Whitman's poem "O Captain! My Captain!" which expressed his sorrow at Lincoln's death.

Bristow's small public library had several books about Lincoln, and I read all of them. By the time I graduated from high school, I had decided that Abraham Lincoln was the greatest American who ever lived. I have never changed that belief.

I saw the Lincoln Memorial, which honors Abraham Lincoln, for the first time during World War II. I had enlisted in the Navy, the new branch called the Seabees, and after basic training was assigned to Camp Peary, near Williamsburg, Virginia. On my first weekend liberty I took a bus to Washington, D.C., only 140 miles (225 kilometers) from Williamsburg, my first visit to the nation's capital. I went to the Capitol Building and the Washington Monument, saw some of the Smithsonian, and stared at the White House through the iron fence. I saved the Lincoln Memorial for last.

In 1943, Washington's beautiful Mall was covered with ugly Quonset huts and temporary prefab buildings necessary to the war effort. But at the end of the Mall stood the Lincoln Memorial, majestic and gleaming in the late afternoon sun. I climbed the sweep of steps leading to the memorial chamber and stood looking up at

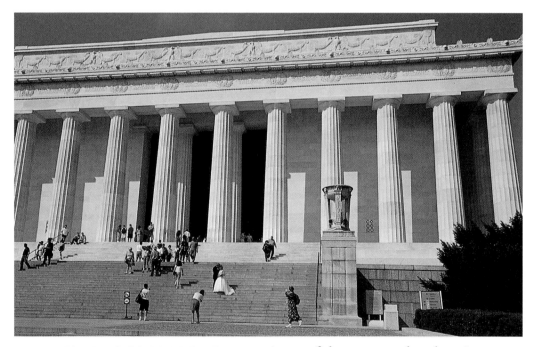

THE LINCOLN MEMORIAL *is one of the most popular places in Washington to pose for a picture.*

THE AUTHOR ENJOYS *one of his favorite views of Washington from the Lincoln Memorial.*

the statue of Lincoln. He seemed quietly thoughtful and comfortable in his great chair. I felt somehow that he was looking at me. Millions of visitors have probably had the feeling I had that day. But at just that moment, in just that light, I was sure that Mr. Lincoln wanted to say something to me.

Sir Winston Churchill once said he thought the Parthenon in Greece, seen by moonlight, to be the most beautiful architectural structure in the world. Some art historians have said that they think India's Taj Mahal is the most beautiful.

I have seen the Parthenon by moonlight. I have seen the Taj Mahal when its marble walls and minarets have been washed to lustrous white by the monsoon rains. The Parthenon and the Taj Mahal are beautiful, breathtakingly so.

But every time I drive across the Potomac River's Memorial Bridge and see the Lincoln Memorial as I enter Washington, my heart rises. After a lifetime, it remains for me the most beautiful structure on earth. Perhaps I feel that way in part because I am an American, and the history behind the memorial is in my blood.

For whatever reason, I am sure of one thing: We are fortunate to have this memorial to greatness as a part of our national heritage.

Brent Ashabranner

CHAPTER ONE
Millennium

EXTENDING FOR ALMOST 2 MILES (3 kilometers) between the U.S. Capitol to the east and the Lincoln Memorial to the west, the Mall is the heart of Washington, D.C. It is a place of walkways, grassy areas, trees, and gardens. Flanking the Mall on both sides are great museums and art galleries: the National Museum of Natural History, the National Air and Space Museum, the National Art Gallery, and many more. Some of our nation's most revered memorials, such as the Vietnam Veterans Memorial and the Korean War Veterans Memorial, are here. A reflecting pool 2,000 feet long and 160 feet wide (610 meters long and 49 meters wide) visually connects the Washington Monument and the Lincoln Memorial. The Mall is an American treasure.

On the cold night of December 31, 1999, more than a hundred thousand people jammed into the Mall from the Washington Monument to the steps of the Lincoln Memorial, which had become a great stage for America's Millennium Gala. It seemed most fitting that the Lincoln Memorial, the nation's best-known symbol of unity and greatness, should have been chosen as the site for a New Year's celebration that would end a century and begin a new thousand years. Giant television screens installed on the Mall would give celebrants a closeup view of the gala events.

THOUSANDS OF PEOPLE *gathered at the Lincoln Memorial to celebrate the new millennium and to watch spectacular fireworks and a magical light show that lasted for many minutes into the new century.*

At ten o'clock the program began with the singing of the National Anthem by Bobby McFerrin. First Lady Hillary Rodham Clinton welcomed the vast throng—and millions of television viewers—and for the next three hours nearly five hundred singers, musicians, dancers, and actors entertained the enthusiastic audience. Among the super all-star cast were Tom Jones, Kenny Rogers, Luther Vandross, Jack Nicholson, Kris Kristofferson, and Mary Tyler Moore. The cast and dancers from the musical *Chicago* performed, as did the cast of *Stomp*. The United States Army Herald Trumpets played. The Symphonic Choir and the World Children's Choir sang.

Timing had to be and was precise. At 11:31 P.M. an eighteen-minute film by Steven Spielberg entitled "The Unfinished Journey" flashed on the giant television screens. With pictures of arriving immigrants, fighting soldiers, construction workers, and scores of other scenes from the century coming to a close, it told the story of the "American Century."

At 11:59 President Bill Clinton took center stage for a brief millennium address. "As we marvel at the changes of the last one hundred years," President Clinton told the crowd, "we dream of

THE CLINTONS
*wave to the crowd
during the Millennium
Gala held in front of
the Lincoln Memorial.*

what changes the next hundred and the next thousand will bring. And as powerful as our memories are, our dreams must be even stronger, for when our memories outweigh our dreams we become old. And it is the eternal destiny of America to remain forever young, always becoming, as our founders pledged, a more appropriate union."

Then President Clinton touched a sparkling torch to a fuse that rocketed, spitting and smoking, the length of the Reflecting Pool. The fuse touched off a spectacular fireworks display that lighted the sky above the Washington Monument and lasted for many minutes into the new century. More music followed, and at 1:52 A.M., January 1, 2000, a fireworks finale and song medley closed America's Millennium Gala.

The marble figure of Abraham Lincoln, relaxed in his massive chair, overlooked the entire gala. In the changing, magical lights of the show, it was not difficult to imagine that, had the great president himself been sitting there on this night, he would have enjoyed what he saw: the people of the nation he died to preserve, united, expressing themselves joyously, facing the new millennium with enthusiasm and hope.

On another day, February 12, less than six weeks into the year 2000, I went to a very different kind of celebration at the Lincoln Memorial. Abraham Lincoln was born on February 12, 1809. Every February 12 since its dedication in 1922, his memorial in Washington has been the place of a commemorative birthday ceremony for him. Today's ceremony, commemorating the 191st anniversary of his birth, had a special feeling because it was the first of the new millennium.

I watched as commemorative wreaths were presented on the memorial steps by the Sons of Union Veterans of the Civil War, the Ladies of the Grand Army of the Republic, the National Order of the Blue and Gray, the Confederate Saltier Association, and more than a dozen other Civil War-related organizations. I listened as the United States Navy Band played "The Battle Cry of Freedom,"

PRESENTATION OF WREATHS *at the observance of Lincoln's 191st birthday.*

"When Johnny Comes Marching Home," and John Phillip Sousa's "The Loyal Legion March." And I stood very still as the words of Abraham Lincoln's Gettysburg Address penetrated the cold early afternoon air.

GETTYSBURG ADDRESS

Four-score and seven years ago, our fathers brought forth upon this continent a new nation, conceived in liberty and dedicated to the proposition that all men are created equal. Now we are engaged in a great civil war, testing whether that nation or any nation so conceived and so dedicated can long endure. We are met on a great battle field of that war. We have come to dedicate a portion of that field, as a final resting place for those who here gave their lives that this nation might live. It is altogether fitting and proper that we should do this. But, in a larger sense, we can not dedicate—we can not consecrate—we can not hallow—this ground. The brave men, living and dead, who struggled here, have consecrated it, far above our poor power to add or detract. The world will little note, nor long remember, what we say here, but it can never forget what they did here. It is for us the living, rather, to be here dedicated to the unfinished work which they who fought here have thus far so nobly advanced. It is rather for us to be here dedicated to the great task remaining before us—that from these honored dead we take increased devotion to that cause for which they gave the last full measure of devotion—that we here highly resolve that these dead shall not have died in vain—that this nation, under God, shall have a new birth of freedom—and that government of the people, by the people, for the people, shall not perish from the earth.

Lincoln's immortal speech, given at the dedication of a national cemetery honoring those who died at the Battle of Gettysburg even as the North and South were still at war, was read on this day by Dr. Jerry C. Bishop, president of the Lincoln Memorial University. A delegation from the university located in Harrogate, Tennessee, also presented a wreath during the wreath ceremony. Lincoln Memorial University came into existence on February 12, 1897, a quarter century before the Lincoln Memorial in Washington, D.C., was built and dedicated. The two have no relationship to each other except that they both grew out of love and respect for Abraham Lincoln.

Although many of its residents opposed slavery, Tennessee seceded from the Union in 1861. Along with Virginia, Tennessee saw some of the bloodiest fighting of the Civil War. Yet within thirty-five years of the war's end, a university honoring Abraham Lincoln's memory was built in Tennessee and to this day serves the people of the state's Cumberland Gap area. Could there be better evidence of the place that the great president had and still has in America's heart?

MANY TOUR GROUPS VISIT *the memorial each year, especially during the spring and summer months.*

AMONG THE MEMORIAL'S FREQUENT VISITORS *are students. These students are awed by the statue of the Great Emancipator.*

Many visitors to the memorial on Lincoln's 191st birthday had not known about the ceremony and were pleased to be there. When the ceremony ended, they climbed the steps to the large memorial chamber to look at Lincoln's statue; to read the words of the Gettysburg Address they had just heard, which are engraved on the south wall; and to look at Lincoln's Second Inaugural Address, which is engraved on the north wall. To see the moving words of the inaugural address carved in stone is to *feel* them in a very special way:

> With malice toward none, with charity for all,
>
> with firmness in the right as God gives us to see the right,
>
> let us finish the work we are in,
>
> to bind up the nation's wounds,
>
> to care for him who shall have borne the battle,
>
> and for his widow and his orphans,
>
> to do all which may achieve and cherish a just and a
>
> lasting peace among ourselves and with all nations.

The chamber was crowded, and I was standing near a young African-American boy and his father. They were both looking up at Lincoln's statue. After perhaps a minute, the boy said, "He sure is big."

The father put his hand on his son's shoulder. "Yes," he said. "He was a big man."

Our national memorials are not only reminders of our nation's heritage. They are also symbols to inspire our quest to become a more perfect union. In the years since its dedication, the Lincoln Memorial has become America's most revered national monument. By best estimates almost 200 million people have visited the memorial.

For most, it is a once-in-a-lifetime experience, a chance to gaze up at Lincoln's serious yet kindly face, to have one's picture taken in front of the colossal statue, to read Lincoln's immortal words, to drink in the incomparable view of the Washington Monument and Capitol beyond the long reflecting pool, to walk to the west side of the memorial and look across the Potomac River at the hills of Arlington National Cemetery, where heroes of every American war are buried.

The very heart of American history is here.

CHAPTER TWO

A Man for the Ages

His work was so colossal, in the face of such discouragement, that none will dispute that he was incomparably the greatest of our presidents.

Thus did President Warren G. Harding assess Abraham Lincoln at the dedication of the Lincoln Memorial in 1922. And although George Washington was "the father of our country" and Franklin D. Roosevelt brought the nation through the Great Depression and the grim first years of World War II, there is little doubt that most Americans would agree with President Harding. It was Lincoln's destiny to save the Union from dismemberment in a terrible Civil War. It was his destiny to end the ugly blight of slavery in America.

Greatness aside, few Americans would disagree that Lincoln has become our most-loved president, whose life, deeds, and words have become a crucial part of our national heritage. Born in a log cabin, Lincoln as a boy worked on his father's farm, read books by firelight to educate himself, became a successful lawyer, and rose to the highest office in the land. His life was the raw material of the American dream in its purest form.

But the heart of the story was yet to come. In 1860, when the Republican Party selected Abraham Lincoln as its candidate for pres-

A PHOTOGRAPH OF PRESIDENT ABRAHAM LINCOLN
taken by a Civil War photographer in 1864.

ident, the United States was a country divided by severe regional differences. A fundamental difference existed between the northern states that advocated the supremacy of federal control and the southern states that believed states rights came first. There was a disagreement about whether slavery would be permitted in western territories that would come into the Union as states. Most alarming to the South was the clamor of abolitionists in the North to make slaveholding illegal in every state in the Union.

During the seventeenth and eighteenth centuries, about five hundred thousand Africans were sold into slavery in North America. The slave trade began with the arrival of a slave ship in Virginia in 1619 and lasted until the importation of slaves was prohibited by federal law in 1808. The 1808 law, however, did not give freedom to enslaved persons already in the country.

The economy of the South was built on slave labor. Production of such money-making crops as rice, cotton, and tobacco increased phenomenally with the growth in the number of slaves. For example, in 1795 the South exported about ten thousand bales of cotton to England. In 1859, when the slave population was at its peak, over *five million* bales were exported. King Cotton had a great appetite for slaves.

Abraham Lincoln never left any doubt about what he thought of the practice of slavery. "He who would *be* no slave must consent to *have no* slave," Lincoln wrote in 1859. "Those who deny freedom to others, deserve it not for themselves, and under a just God cannot long retain it." And in words that could not be clearer, he said, "If slavery is not wrong, nothing is wrong."

Lincoln held a series of famous debates with Stephen Douglas, an Illinois senator who wanted to be president and who believed that each state had the right to decide whether slavery was legal. In one of the debates, Lincoln said, "There is no reason in the world why the Negro is not entitled to all the natural rights enumerated in the Declaration of Independence, the right to life, liberty, and the pursuit of happiness. I hold that he is as much entitled to these as the white man."

In the presidential election of 1860, the Democratic ticket was split between the Northern Democrats who nominated Stephen Douglas and the Southern Democrats who, unwilling to accept any Northerner, nominated John C. Breckenridge of Kentucky. With the Democratic vote divided, Lincoln was swept into office by winning every northern state.

Although he was morally opposed to slavery, Lincoln, even before he became president, sought to reassure the South that he had no intention of trying to pass a law making the owning of slaves illegal. His policy would first be to attempt to prevent the spread of slavery to the new territories and then to find ways to compensate southern slave owners who freed their slaves.

Unconvinced, South Carolina seceded from the Union on December 20, 1860, more than two months before Abraham Lincoln was to take the oath of office as president. The state announced that it was now a sovereign nation dedicated to the preservation of slavery. Six other southern states quickly followed and with South Carolina formed the Confederate States of America.

On March 4, 1861, standing in front of the Capitol in Washington, D.C., Abraham Lincoln was sworn in as the sixteenth president of the United States. He continued to hope that the southern states that had seceded would return voluntarily to the Union, and that day he spoke to them:

> In *your* hands, my dissatisfied countrymen, and not in mine, is the momentous issue of civil war. The government will not assail *you*. *You* can have no conflict, without being yourselves the aggressors. *You* have no oath registered in Heaven to destroy the government, while I shall have the most solemn one to "preserve, protect, and defend" it.

Five weeks later, on April 12, the Confederate States gave President Lincoln their answer. On that day, rebel cannons opened fire on Fort Sumter, a federal-government fort in Charleston Harbor, South Carolina. The savage bombardment continued for thirty-six hours until the fort surrendered. Four other southern states joined the Confederacy, and the American Civil War had begun.

Officials in Washington, D.C., even President Lincoln, believed that the war would end quickly. After all, the North had twenty-three states with a total population of 22 million and great military, industrial, and financial resources. The South had eleven states, about 9 million people—over a third of them slaves—and essentially a farming economy. Surely the southern states would soon be forced to return to the Union.

But the South had a fierce determination to protect its way of life, and the Confederacy had a resource the Union did not have: a great store of military talent. Jefferson Davis, the newly elected president of the Confederate States of America, had previously been U.S. secretary of war. Robert E. Lee, commander of the army of Northern Virginia and later general-in-chief of all Confederate forces, is considered by many historians the greatest Civil War general. The South had other outstanding generals as well, such as Thomas Jonathan "Stonewall" Jackson and James Ewell Brown (Jeb) Stuart, a superb cavalry leader.

In the first year of the war, the South won repeated victories on Virginia battlefields: the First Battle of Bull Run; on the York Peninsula; in the Shenandoah Valley; at the town of Fredericksburg, where the Union army lost twelve thousand men; the Second Battle of Bull Run ("We are whipped again!" lamented President Lincoln).

The president struggled with scant success to find competent generals to lead the Union armies. He began to fear that the war was lost. Many in the northern states, dismayed and discouraged by Union losses, wanted to let the southern states go their separate way rather than wage war to keep them in the Union. But northern abolitionists continued to press for war to free the slaves.

In a famous open letter to Horace Greeley, the editor of *The New York Tribune,* in August 1862, Lincoln answered both the abolitionists and those who thought secession should not be resisted. "My paramount object in this struggle is to save the Union," Lincoln wrote, "and is not either to save or to destroy slavery. What I do about slavery and the colored race, I do because I believe it will help save the Union."

In fact, Lincoln had already decided that issuing a proclamation freeing the slaves in the rebellious states would be a severe blow to the Confederacy, but he felt he must wait until the North had won a victory on the battlefield. Otherwise, the proclamation would seem like a desperate and meaningless gesture.

The agonizing wait for a victory was about to end. In September 1862 General Robert E. Lee led his rebel forces northward into Maryland. There, at a little stream called Antietam Creek they were confronted by a large Union army under the command of General George McClellan. On September 17, the bloodiest day of the entire Civil War, twenty-five thousand men, from both the North and the South, were killed or wounded. But the Union lines held, and Lee and his troops were forced to retreat back to Virginia.

Antietam was an incomplete victory at best, because McClellan did not pursue the retreating Lee. But it gave Lincoln, using the presidential war powers to weaken the enemy any way he could, the opportunity to issue an executive order—on September 22—freeing all slaves in the rebellious states unless those states returned to the Union by January 1, 1863. No Confederate state did return to the Union by that date. On January 1, 1863, Lincoln signed the Emancipation Proclamation, freeing all slaves in the Confederate States of America "henceforth and forever."

The immediate effect of the Emancipation Proclamation was to give the North a new goal: to restore a Union without slavery. Another effect was to gain support for the Union cause abroad, especially in Great Britain, which had outlawed slavery in 1833.

While the Emancipation Proclamation could be enforced in the rebellious states only with Union military success, the ultimate effect as the war progressed was to deplete the human resources of the Confederacy, and add strength to the Union. As word of emancipation filtered through the South, slaves escaped in increasing numbers, often finding refuge with Union military forces. Blacks who wished to volunteer could now enlist in the Union army, and thousands did. By the time the war ended, almost two hundred thousand blacks, most of them emancipated slaves, were wearing the Union-army blue.

Lincoln knew that the Emancipation Proclamation would in time have to be supported by a Constitutional amendment making slavery illegal not only in the rebellious states but in every state; the loyal slaveholding border states had not been affected by the Emancipation Proclamation. Lincoln would work hard for such an amendment—the Thirteenth Amendment to the Constitution—which was passed by the House of Representatives in January 1865 and ratified, or approved, by the states later that year.

THE EMANCIPATION PROCLAMATION

Whereas, on the twenty-second day of September, in the year of our Lord one thousand eight hundred and sixty-two, a proclamation was issued by the President of the United States, containing, among other things, the following, to wit:

> That on the first day of January, in the year of our Lord one thousand eight hundred and sixty-three, all persons held as slaves within any State or designated part of a State, the people whereof shall then be in rebellion against the United States, shall be then, thenceforward, and forever free; and the Executive Government of the United States, including the military and naval authority thereof, will recognize and maintain the freedom of such persons, and will do no act or acts to repress such persons, or any of them, in any efforts they may make for their actual freedom.

> That the Executive will, on the first day of January aforesaid, by proclamation, designate the States and parts of States, if any, in which the people thereof, respectively, shall then be in rebellion against the United States; and the fact that any State, or the people thereof, shall on that day be, in good faith, represented in the Congress of the United States by members chosen thereto at elections wherein a majority of the qualified voters of such State shall have participated, shall, in the absence of strong countervailing testimony, be deemed conclusive evidence that such State, and the people thereof, are not then in rebellion against the United States.

Now, therefore I, Abraham Lincoln, President of the United States, by virtue of the power in me vested as Commander-in-Chief, of the Army and Navy of the United States in time of actual armed rebellion against the authority and government of the United States, and as a fit and necessary war measure for suppressing said rebellion, do, on this first day of January, in the year of our Lord one thousand eight hundred and sixty-three, and in accordance with my purpose so to do publicly proclaimed for the full Period of one hundred days, from the day first above mentioned, order and designate as the States and parts of States wherein the people thereof respectively, are this day in rebellion against the United States, the following, to wit:

Arkansas, Texas, Louisiana, (except the Parishes of St. Bernard, Plaquemines, Jefferson, St. John, St. Charles, St James Ascension, Assumption, Terrebonne, Lafourche, St. Mary, St. Martin, and Orleans, including the city of New Orleans) Mississippi, Alabama, Florida, Georgia, South Carolina, North Carolina, and Virginia, (except the forty-eight counties designated as West Virginia, and also the counties of Berkley, Accomac, Northampton, Elizabeth City, York, Princess Ann, and Norfolk, including the cities of Norfolk and Portsmouth), and which excepted part, are for the present, left precisely as if this proclamation were not issued.

And by virtue of the power, and for the purpose aforesaid, I do order and declare that all persons held as slaves within said designated States, and parts of States, are, and henceforward shall be free; and that the Executive government of the United States, including the military and naval authorities thereof, will recognize and maintain the freedom of said persons.

And I hereby enjoin upon the people so I declared to be free to abstain from all violence, unless in necessary self-defence; and I recommend to them that, in all cases when allowed, they labor faithfully for reasonable wages.

And I further declare and make known, that such persons of suitable condition will be received into the armed service of the United States to garrison forts, positions, stations, and other places, and to man vessels of all sorts in said service.

And upon this act, sincerely believed to be an act of justice, warranted by the Constitution, upon military necessity, I invoke the considerate judgment of mankind, and the gracious favor of Almighty God.

The war raged on for more than two years after the signing of the Emancipation Proclamation, taking a great toll on the careworn president. Throughout his years of leadership he was beset by problems of finding able military commanders, by a critical and uncooperative Congress, by a cabinet divided by internal hatreds, and by a national press that assailed him as a tyrant, a stupid bungler in military affairs, a coward, a backwoods hick. Lincoln bore these problems and attacks with a calm patience. In the darkest days of the war, when the outcome was perilously in doubt, he wrote these words, which were found among his papers after his death: "If the end brings me out all right, what is said against me will not amount to anything. If the end brings me out all wrong, ten angels swearing I was right would make no difference."

By early 1865, Lincoln knew that the end was going to bring him out all right. At last a strong general-in-chief of Union armies had emerged: Ulysses S. Grant. Slowly the Union armies had ground down those of the Confederacy. On a quiet Sunday, the ninth of April, Robert E. Lee surrendered the army of Northern Virginia to Grant at Appomattox Courthouse. The terrible Civil War that had taken almost half a million lives from the North and South was effectively over. The states would be one Union again. Slavery had been abolished in the South, and soon a Constitutional amendment would make the owning of a human being by another human being a crime in every state. Many of the president's severest critics were beginning to change their minds about him.

The man who had borne the nation's tragedy on his shoulders and its sorrow in his heart knew a measure of peace at last. In a book about Lincoln, John Nicolay, one of his two confidential secretaries, told of a talk the president had with his wife during a carriage ride on Good Friday afternoon, April 14.

"Mary," Lincoln said, "we have had a hard time of it since we came to Washington, but the war is over, and with God's blessing we may hope for four years of peace and happiness, and then we will go back to Illinois and pass the rest of our lives in quiet."

AN INSCRIPTION CARVED IN STONE *over Lincoln's statue inside the memorial built to honor him reads, "In this temple, as in the hearts of the people for whom he saved the Union, the memory of Abraham Lincoln is enshrined forever." Written by Royal Cortissoz, who served for fifty years as art critic of* The New York Tribune, *the inscription attests to the great love Americans continue to feel for Lincoln. Although Cortissoz wrote many highly regarded biographies and books of art criticism, he always said that he was proudest of this one-sentence inscription.*

That night, while enjoying a performance of a comedy, *Our American Cousin*, at Ford's Theater a few blocks from the White House, Lincoln was shot by John Wilkes Booth. He died the next morning without regaining consciousness.

People across the country were stunned. In every city they gathered in huge, silent crowds in front of newspaper offices and telegraph offices to wait for the latest word. Many refused to believe what they read or heard. They remembered Lincoln's gaunt, sad face. They remembered the way he had held the Union steadily on course. They remembered his clear, simple words at Gettysburg that made them understand why they had to endure such a cruel civil war. In the few hours between the fatal shot on Good Friday and the coming of Easter Sunday, the seeds of Abraham Lincoln as man, myth, and American folk hero took root forever.

On Monday evening Lincoln's embalmed body was placed in a large coffin and carried to the East Room of the White House. On Tuesday the White House was opened so that people could pay their last respects to the fallen leader. For eight hours, tens of thousands of men, women, and children filed past the coffin, pausing for not more than a few seconds to look down at Lincoln's face.

A funeral service was held in the East Room on Wednesday. Then Lincoln's body lay in state in the Capitol rotunda, again to be viewed by thousands. On Friday morning it began its long train journey to Springfield, Illinois, where interment would take place. The route would retrace almost exactly that over which Lincoln traveled to Washington after being elected president in 1860, a route of 1,700 miles (2,737 kilometers), passing through many of the large cities of the East and Midwest. In each city Lincoln's coffin was taken from the train, and a massive public funeral was held.

At last, on May 3, the train reached Springfield, where the final funeral and ceremonies were held. On the morning of May 4, General Joseph Hooker, one of Lincoln's wartime generals, led a long procession to Oak Ridge Cemetery, where Lincoln's coffin was placed beside a smaller one that was already there. That coffin held the body of the Lincolns' beloved son Willie, who had died in the White House at the age of eleven.

CHAPTER THREE

A Memorial for Mr. Lincoln

HARDLY HAD THE LAST FUNERAL been held for the martyred president than friends and admirers began to call for a memorial in his honor. In March 1867, less than two years after his death, Congress created a Lincoln Memorial Association. The association immediately invited Clark Mills, the most famous American sculptor of his day, to submit his ideas for a monument to Lincoln. Among Mills's many public sculptures, one of the most famous is the statue of Andrew Jackson on horseback in Lafayette Square, in front of the White House.

Sculptor Mills quickly presented to the association his design for a memorial to Lincoln. His plans called for a monument 70 feet (21 meters) high topped by a huge figure of Lincoln. The president would be surrounded by thirty-one foot soldiers and six mounted cavalrymen, all of "colossal size."

The association accepted Mills's design, and in so doing revealed the intense feelings of resentment that prevailed in the aftermath of the Civil War. The men of the association, all Northerners, wanted to portray Lincoln as a conquering war hero who had crushed the rebellious states of the Confederacy. They had no interest in showing the forgiving, humanitarian side of the great president.

THANKS TO ILLINOIS SENATOR SHELBY CULLOM *and others, Congress finally passed a bill authorizing the building of a memorial to Abraham Lincoln in 1911. Here a high school choir from Sumter, South Carolina, begins a concert on the Reflecting Pool terrace in front of the memorial.*

Congress had appropriated no money to build the monument, instead planning to call for voluntary contributions from the public. But the plan was never publicized, and almost no money was collected. As a result, Mills's monument was never built. In time, the Lincoln Monument Association ceased to exist, and Mills's memorial design was forgotten.

A memorial to Abraham Lincoln might have been forgotten forever had it not been for the efforts of Illinois Senator Shelby Cullom. Senator Cullom had known Lincoln well and had admired him as a great and humane leader. Cullom tried for years to guide a Lincoln Memorial bill through the Senate but failed repeatedly. Now old and in ill health, Senator Cullom knew that his time in the Senate and, indeed, his time on earth, was short.

In 1910, Senator Cullom enlisted the aid of Congressman Joseph Cannon, powerful speaker of the House of Representatives and also an admirer of Lincoln. Together the two men pushed a Lincoln Memorial bill through both the House and the Senate, and it was signed into law by President William Howard Taft on February 19, 1911. According to Smith D. Fry, the historian of the Capitol at the time, Senator Cullom, upon hearing that Taft had signed the bill, said, "Now, Lord, let thy servant depart in peace."

Almost half a century had passed since Lincoln's death, but the new bill ensured that a memorial to the Great Emancipator would now be built. Not only did the new bill appropriate two million dollars—a considerable amount of money in 1911—it also named President Taft himself as chairman of a Lincoln Memorial Commission.

The commission was quickly deluged with ideas about what the memorial should be and where it should be located. Congressman James McCleary of Minnesota proposed that the memorial take the form of a 200-foot-wide highway (61 meters wide) between Washington, D.C., and Gettysburg, with patriotic statues and other memorials to Lincoln along the way. Some groups wanted a glorious Abraham Lincoln memorial park in the nation's capital; others wanted a monumental triumphal arch at some main entrance to the city. Most suggestions were to place the memorial in Washington in the middle of the city, perhaps near the Union Railway Station or the Capitol. Some groups wanted the memorial to be in Springfield, Illinois, Gettysburg, or other locations made famous by the Civil War.

The Lincoln Memorial Commission listened to all suggestions but came to its own very firm conclusions. First, the memorial must contain a statue of Lincoln. Second, the statue must be contained in an appropriate architectural structure. Third, the memorial should be located in Washington, D.C., but not in the busy center of the city.

The National Park Service wanted the Lincoln Memorial to be built in a part of Washington known as Potomac Park. It was an area of the Potomac River tidal basin that had been marshy, swampy land before it had been drained and filled between 1882-1902. The area was still barren, treeless, and forlorn, but there were those who saw

A VIEW FROM *the west side of the Lincoln Memorial across the Potomac's Memorial Bridge to Robert E. Lee's home, "Arlington House," in Arlington National Cemetery.*

it as an ideal location for a memorial to Lincoln. John Hay, one of President Lincoln's personal secretaries and later secretary of state, wrote: "His memorial should stand alone, remote from the common habitations of man, apart from the business and turmoil of the city, isolated, distinguished, and serene."

In the end, the most effective argument was that the Potomac Park site would put the Lincoln Memorial on an axis of the Capitol and the Washington Monument. Thus it would face the monument to the nation's first president and the Capitol of the nation that Lincoln gave his life to preserve.

In February 1912 the Lincoln Memorial Commission agreed that Potomac Park would be the site of the Lincoln Memorial. The next tasks were to find the right architect and the right sculptor to create the memorial.

CHAPTER FOUR
Creating the Memorial:
Henry Bacon

FROM THE BEGINNING of the Lincoln Memorial Commission's search for an architect to design the memorial, one name stood out: that of Henry Bacon. In many ways Henry Bacon's life seems to have been an almost uncanny preparation to design and build the great memorial. He was born in 1866, the year after Lincoln's death, and grew up in the years when the Civil War and Lincoln were still topics of daily discussion everywhere in the country.

From his father, a civil engineer who built railroads and bridges, Bacon even as a boy became fascinated with the way things were designed. By the time he finished secondary school, he had made up his mind that he wanted to be an architect. He enrolled at the University of Illinois but left after only a year. In late-nineteenth-century America, the way to become an architect was to work and study in a good architectural firm.

Bacon was accepted as an apprentice draftsman in an architectural firm in Boston. He did so well there that he was soon invited to join McKim, Mead, and White, at that time the leading firm of architects in America. One of the partners, Charles Follen McKim, had a deep love of classical Greek and Roman architecture, which he quickly passed on to the new young man in the office.

HENRY BACON

At the age of twenty-three, Bacon won a scholarship that paid all expenses for two years of travel and study in Europe. In Greece he fell under the spell of the Parthenon, the sculpture from the temple of Zeus, and other marvels of Greek architecture and sculpture. This appreciation would be a guiding force throughout his life as an architect.

Back in America, Bacon rejoined McKim, Mead, and White as a full-fledged architect. He worked on the design and construction of many important public buildings in New York and other Eastern cities. In 1892 plans were well in progress for a huge Chicago World's Fair to celebrate the four-hundredth anniversary of Columbus's discovery of America. The plans called for the creation of many monumental buildings in the classical tradition to house exhibits from all over the world. The firm of McKim, Mead, and White was called in to design the buildings, and Henry Bacon was sent to Chicago as executive architect to oversee the huge project. Unknow-

THE PARTHENON, *often considered the greatest masterpiece of Greek architecture, inspired Henry Bacon's vision of the Lincoln Memorial.*

ingly, young Bacon had taken another step toward his destiny as creator of a memorial to Abraham Lincoln.

The Chicago World's Fair was a great success; and the magnificence of the White City, as the Fair's buildings were called, greatly enhanced Henry Bacon's stature as an architect. In 1897 Bacon left McKim, Mead, and White and practiced under his own name for the rest of his life.

From the time of his studies in Greece, Bacon had been deeply interested in the combination of architecture and sculpture. In pursuit of this interest he began to work with Daniel Chester French, a sculptor of growing reputation who had also worked at the World's Fair. Over time, Bacon and French formed a professional relationship and a close friendship. Together they worked on at least fifty monuments and memorials, such as the monuments to Henry Wadsworth Longfellow in Cambridge, Massachusetts, and to James Oglethorpe, founder of the Georgia colony, in Savannah, Georgia. Most significant in terms of their future work together was their collaboration in 1911 on an Abraham Lincoln monument for the state capitol grounds in Lincoln, Nebraska.

In early 1912 the Lincoln Memorial Commission invited Bacon to submit a tentative design for the Lincoln Memorial to be built in

Washington, D.C. Bacon felt greatly honored, although he knew that the invitation did not necessarily mean that he would be selected to be the memorial's architect. John Russell Pope, another well-known American architect, also submitted memorial designs.

Bacon immediately began to give intense thought to the memorial and made experimental sketches. He was aware of the report of a committee that had been appointed by the U.S. Senate in 1901 to make recommendations for the future erection of public buildings and monuments in Washington. About a possible Lincoln Memorial the committee had written: "Whatever may be the exact form selected for the memorial to Lincoln, in type it should possess the quality of universality, and also it should have a character essentially different from that of any monument either existing in the District or hereafter to be erected."

In other words, the committee wanted something very different for a memorial to Lincoln and something that would not be copied in the future. One of the committee members had been Charles Follen McKim, the architect who had guided Bacon to his love of Greek architecture. Bacon was sure that in the term "universality," McKim was thinking, at least in part, about the classic architecture of the Greeks and Romans.

Bacon also knew that the Lincoln Memorial Commission had previously set down ideas about the memorial. They wanted to avoid any competition with the Washington Monument and the Capitol. Therefore, they said, the Lincoln Memorial should not have great height such as the Washington Monument had, nor should it have a dome that might remind viewers of the Capitol. Bacon agreed with all of the commission's thoughts.

Bacon submitted his plans and designs in the fall of 1912. Approval came quickly from the Lincoln Memorial Commission and from Congress, and on February 1, 1913, the President gave the final approval. That same day the Lincoln Memorial Commission named Henry Bacon to be the architect of the memorial.

Bacon's conception of the memorial was masterful in its blending of grandeur and simplicity. His plans projected a memorial that appealed to the emotions with a statue of the great president in a noble setting. In his notes, Bacon wrote "The most important object is the statue of Lincoln, which is placed in the center of the Memorial, and by virtue of its imposing position in the place of honor, the gentleness, power, and intelligence of the man, expressed as far as possible by the sculptor's art, predominates."

But in Bacon's vision, the memorial should appeal not only to the heart but also to the head, the intellect. To that end he specified that Lincoln's wise and beautifully expressed words, which had given the Union courage and a sense of purpose, should be an integral part of the memorial. The figure of Lincoln would be in a large central chamber; his Gettysburg Address and his Second Inaugural Address would be engraved on the walls of smaller flanking chambers.

Bacon's plans also called for two huge colorful murals to be placed high above the great speeches in the smaller north and south chambers. The murals would symbolize Lincoln's emancipation of the American slaves and his triumph in preserving the Union.

The memorial structure Bacon envisioned to contain Lincoln's statue would be a modified Greek temple. Bacon turned the temple so that its side was at right angles to the Mall; this created the desired

THE LINCOLN MEMORIAL *on a summer day. The east facade faces the Reflecting Pool and the Washington Monument.*

THE NAMES OF THE THIRTY-SIX STATES *in the Union at the time of Lincoln's death are inscribed on the frieze above the memorial's colonnade. The dates of statehood appear in Roman numerals.*

"strong horizontal lines" and served as a forceful terminus to the western end of the Mall.

In Bacon's design, the central block of the memorial containing the statues, the texts, and the murals would be enclosed by thirty-six columns forming a surrounding porch representing the thirty-six states in the Union at the time of Lincoln's death. The names of the states would be cut into the frieze or sculptured band above the colonnade, the columns supporting the roof. Another departure from the Greek temple form would be a recessed attic, corresponding in size to that of the chamber block below. The outer wall of the attic would be decorated with the names of the forty-eight states that comprised the United States at the time the Lincoln Memorial was built.

Bacon saw in the memorial structure, the statue of Lincoln, Lincoln's immortal words, and the symbolic murals a perfect coming together of architecture, art, literature, and history.

Not everyone was pleased with Henry Bacon's plans for the Lincoln Memorial. His plans stirred up controversy among artists, architects, historians, and just plain people who had their own feelings about Lincoln. The main criticism was that a Greek temple was not appropriate for a man of Lincoln's humble log cabin origins, a plain-speaking American folk hero, a down-to-earth man of the people. His statue would look out of place there, many people said, uncomfortable, untrue.

Bacon, however, also had many supporters. Among the first to speak in defense of the modified Greek temple was his friend Daniel Chester French. "The memorial tells you just what manner of man you are come to pay homage to," French wrote; "his simplicity, his grandeur, and his power."

Aware of controversy but believing in his own vision, Bacon prepared the detailed drawings necessary for constructing the memorial. Work on the structure began early in 1914, and for the next eight years—for the rest of his life, in fact—the Lincoln Memorial became Bacon's absorbing interest. Every detail of construction was carried out under his watchful eyes. He never had any doubt that the Lincoln Memorial would be the crowning achievement of his rich life in architecture.

HENRY BACON *had American boxwood and holly planted around the memorial to soften its formality and provide a feeling of warmth.*

ABOUT THE LINCOLN MEMORIAL

To build the massive memorial on drained and filled
Potomac River land required the most stable of subfoundations.
To assure that stability, 122 solid poured-concrete piers
with steel reinforcing rods were driven to bedrock
at depths of 44 to 65 feet (13.4 to 19.8 meters).

The height of the memorial's great superstructure is
79 feet 10 inches (24.3 meters) from the top of
the foundation to the top of the attic.

The columns in the colonnade are 44 feet
(13.4 meters) from top to bottom.

The interior columns that divide the three chambers
of the memorial are 50 feet (15.2 meters) from
the floor to the top of the cap.

The central chamber containing Lincoln's statue is 60 feet
(18.3 meters) wide and 74 feet (22.6 meters) deep.
The two side chambers containing Lincoln's speeches
are 60 feet (18.3 meters) wide and 38 feet (11.6 meters) deep.

The memorial is built of a variety of materials, including marble,
granite, limestone, brick, and concrete. The exterior of the building is built of white Colorado marble. The interior walls and
columns are made of Indiana limestone. The interior floor,
which is 2 inches (5 centimeters) thick, and the wall base
are of pink Tennessee marble. The ceiling, 60 feet (18.3 meters)
above the floor, is made of bronze beams and panels of
Alabama marble about one inch (2.5 centimeters) thick.

The statue of Abraham Lincoln was carved
from white Georgia marble.

The total cost of building the memorial was $2,957,000.
The total cost of Lincoln's statue was $88,400.

CHAPTER FIVE

Creating Lincoln's Statue:
Daniel Chester French

IN 1914 THE LINCOLN MEMORIAL Commission chose Daniel Chester French to sculpt the statue of Lincoln for the memorial. French was almost seventeen years older than Bacon and did not begin what was to be the great work of his life until he was sixty-four years old. Born in 1850, the youngest of four children in a well-to-do New England family, he was fifteen by the time the Civil War ended, old enough to have known men going into and returning from battle, old enough to have read the words of Lincoln's Gettysburg Address in the Boston newspapers.

After secondary school, French had no desire to go to college. He did some work on the family farm and, with plenty of spare time, began to make clay figures of animals: dogs, cats, and wild creatures—fulfilling a deeply felt urge to create. May Alcott, a neighbor of the Frenches and sister of the famous author of *Little Women*, heard about Daniel French's clay figures and came to look at them. She was astonished at his natural talent. Herself an artist and art teacher, May Alcott gave French drawing lessons and some sculptor's tools, and told him to keep working.

French did keep working. He went to New York to study sculpture but returned to the family farm after only a few months, dissatisfied with city life. Unexpectedly, French's homecoming turned

DANIEL CHESTER FRENCH *in his studio at Chesterwood, his home in Stockbridge, Massachusetts. A model of the Lincoln statue is in the background.*

out to be a move that launched his artistic career. The nearby town of Concord, where the first battle of the Revolutionary War had been fought, wanted to erect a statue to a Minuteman for its centennial celebration in 1875, less than two years away. The Concord statue committee asked French if he would like to submit a model for the statue.

He would! French went to work feverishly on drawings, and in a month presented a small clay model to the committee. They liked what they saw and gave French his first commission as a professional sculptor.

French worked for months, often ten hours a day, beginning with a 3-foot (1-meter) clay model on which he labored to get just the right pose. In this cradle of the American Revolutionary War, French discovered that his neighbors could find in their attics everything he needed to guide his work: authentic Minuteman clothes, a colonial-period musket and powder horn, even a hundred-year-old plow—for as French conceived his statue, the Minuteman was a farmer who carried a gun to defend his country.

When French finished his model in clay, it was cast in plaster and then in bronze by professional casters in Boston. From the moment of its unveiling, the Minuteman was a great success. Since its dedication it has guarded North Bridge, Concord, with an air of sturdy defiance, just as the bridge was guarded in 1776 by colonists who were ready to drop their plows and fight British troops at a minute's notice.

After completing the Minuteman, French studied classical Roman sculpture in Italy for a short time but remained essentially a self-taught artist. His progress in a career as a sculptor was leisurely. By the time he was forty, he had executed only seven statues for display in public parks and buildings, but they included some outstanding work. Among them were a bust of Ralph Waldo Emerson and a statue of the ancient Greek historian Herodotus for the Library of Congress in Washington, D.C.

Although his body of work was small, its quality was such that French was asked to take part in preparations for the World's Fair in Chicago in 1893. The opportunities for sculpture at the great exhibition opened the gates of his creative energy reservoir. During the remainder of his life, French created 120 statues and other sculptures for buildings and parks all over the United States.

The selection of Daniel French to sculpt the statue of Abraham Lincoln for the Lincoln Memorial brought him together once more with Bacon for what would be their last and greatest collaboration. From the very beginning their goal was to bring about a perfect unity of statue and building.

French went immediately to Washington to see the still-unfinished memorial building and was awed by the great templelike structure of gleaming white marble that his friend had designed. And to think that it was being built to contain but a single statue!

In their first talks Bacon and French made two important decisions. The first was that the figure of Lincoln had to be seated. A standing figure would put Lincoln's head too far above the eye of a person inside the memorial. The second decision was that Lincoln should not be seated in an armchair such that he might have used during his lifetime. Such chair would be informal, too "folksy." They decided on a curule chair, the type of massive, formal chair in which only the highest officers of Roman antiquity were privileged to sit. Such a chair would provide the proper dignity for Lincoln without giving any appearance that he was sitting on a throne.

French returned to his home and studio, called "Chesterwood," in a lovely rural area near Stockbridge, Massachusetts. For the next three years he was totally absorbed in creating Lincoln's statue. He studied photographs that had been taken of the president during his lifetime. He reviewed notes he had taken during several talks with Robert Lincoln, the president's only living son. He pored over photographs of the many statues of Lincoln that already existed, some by prominent sculptors. These projected Lincoln in many ways: the railsplitter, the orator, the young lawyer, the emancipator. They showed him praying, dying, surrounded by his generals, seated on horseback. Some of the statues were well done, some poorly done, but they all made a statement about some phase of Lincoln's life.

That was not what Daniel French wanted. He wanted his statue of Lincoln to be Lincoln the president, the humanitarian, the preserver of the Union. He wanted the burdens of Civil War to show in the president's rugged features.

Finally, French began to put his research and thought into clay and made a small-scale model in which his first concern was form—the shape and composition of the sculpture. He liked the result, and so did Henry Bacon and the Lincoln Memorial Commission. French then made a 3-foot (1-meter) clay model in which he paid special attention to Lincoln's hands and head and the position of his feet. French had always felt that hands are especially expressive of personality. He symbolized Lincoln's strength and determination with a clenched left hand and his calm nature with a relaxed right hand.

By the end of 1916, French had completed work on a 7-foot (2-meter) enlargement of the model, now striving to show the power he sensed in the bony ruggedness of Lincoln's face and to add

FRENCH ADDED *drapery to Lincoln's chair to soften its hard lines.*

a look of thoughtful concern to the careworn features. He made certain that Lincoln's clothes were exactly of the type he would have worn in the 1860s.

French made trips to Washington to work with Bacon in determining the exact size that the finished statue would be. After numerous experiments with photographic enlargements glued to fiberboard, they decided the statue should be 19 feet (5.8 meters) high measuring from Lincoln's foot to the top of his head and that the statue should sit on a pedestal elevated 11 feet (3.6 meters) high. They also concluded that the statue would be made of white marble rather than bronze, because bronze would appear too dark in the memorial chamber.

THE STATUE OF LINCOLN *being assembled at the Lincoln Memorial.*

Now the time had come to bring others into work. French went to New York in 1918 to engage the services of the Piccirilli brothers, an Italian-American family whose marble-cutting skills had made them famous. The statue of Lincoln was so huge that there was no possibility of quarrying one block of marble from which to cut it. Instead twenty-eight separate blocks were used.

The art of the marble cutter now took over. Using techniques as ancient as those of Michelangelo, the Piccirilli brothers cut the Lincoln statue from the blocks, with French's 7-foot (2-meter) model as their guide. During the year the carving took, French spent much of his time in the Piccirilli workshop adding his personal touch with hammer and chisel.

The blocks of the statue were shipped to Washington, and in December 1920 their assembling began, like the pieces of a giant puzzle. So perfect was the work of the Piccirilli brothers that any seam between the blocks was almost invisible. When the statue was in place in the memorial, French again took his sculptor's tools and added final refinements to his masterpiece.

"It is now as technically perfect as I can make it," French said.

And, as tens of millions of memorial visitors have seen, the Lincoln statue was more than technically perfect. It was also as artistically perfect as a great sculptor's genius could make it.

CHAPTER SIX
What the Lincoln Memorial Means to America

LIKE NO OTHER NATIONAL MEMORIAL before or since, the Lincoln Memorial has taken a special place in the hearts and minds of Americans. It has become a symbol of hope that America's leaders will find within themselves some of Lincoln's qualities of greatness. It has become a symbol of the "patient confidence" that Lincoln had in the wisdom and courage of the common people. More than anything else, it has become a symbol of the founding fathers' declaration that everyone is created equal in the right to pursue a happy life. In his speeches, his writings, his actions, Abraham Lincoln kept that fundamental truth before the American people.

At certain moments in the twentieth century the symbolic power of the Lincoln Memorial has been forcefully felt. In 1939 the black American singer Marian Anderson was scheduled to give a concert in Washington, D.C. The concert sponsor wanted her performance to be in Constitution Hall, at that time Washington's best concert facility. Miss Anderson was one of the great contraltos of her time, or of any time. Despite her talent and despite the fact that she had sung in the great concert halls of Europe for years, the owners of Constitution Hall, the Daughters of the American Revolution (DAR), refused to let the great contralto sing in their building. The DAR policy, they said, was that Constitution Hall was available to

ON OCTOBER 11, 1954, *Marian Anderson sang again at the Lincoln Memorial on the occasion of a memorial service for Harold L. Ickes, who died in 1952. As Secretary of the Interior, Ickes approved Ms. Anderson's concert at the Lincoln Memorial.*

white artists only. The United States was still a racially segregated nation in 1939, but so renowned was Marian Anderson as a singer that an outcry against the DAR policy was heard all over the country. Eleanor Roosevelt, wife of President Franklin D. Roosevelt, resigned in protest from the DAR when that organization would not change its position on Miss Anderson's concert.

In a solution that made history, the federal government agreed to let Marian Anderson's concert be held at the Lincoln Memorial. When Miss Anderson walked onto the steps of the memorial at five o'clock in the afternoon of April 9, an audience of seventy-five thousand had come to hear her.

The great contralto paused and turned to look at the statue of Abraham Lincoln behind her. Then she took her place behind a battery of microphones, closed her eyes, and in a voice choked with emotion, began to sing. Her opening number was "America," and the first words, "My country 'tis of thee, sweet land of liberty," brought a complete hush over the vast audience.

Marian Anderson's dramatic performance in the symbolic setting of the Lincoln Memorial that April afternoon helped to focus national attention on the ugly reality of racial inequality in America as it had seldom been focused before.

Twenty-four years later, on August 28, 1963, a quarter of a million people gathered in Washington, D.C., for a great civil rights demonstration. Named the "March on Washington for Jobs and Freedom," it was led by Dr. Martin Luther King Jr. and both blacks and whites came from every state in the nation to take part.

At the Lincoln Memorial that day, Dr. King spoke to the civil rights marchers and to millions of radio and television listeners. Standing only a few feet from the statue of the Great Emancipator, Dr. King called the Lincoln Memorial "this hallowed spot," and he spoke against "the manacles of segregation and the chains of discrimination."

But mainly he spoke of his dream that the nation would listen to and begin to live by the words of the Declaration of Independence: "We hold these truths to be self-evident; that all men are created equal." He spoke of his dream of an America where people "will not be judged by the color of their skin but by the content of their character." He spoke of his dream of a day when the black and white people of this country "will be able to work together, to pray together, to struggle together." If America was to become a truly great nation, he said, these things must happen. Dr. King's moving plea at the Lincoln Memorial has become known as his "I Have a Dream" speech.

THE CROWD IN FRONT *of the Lincoln Memorial grew to 250,000 on August 28, 1963, as they waited to hear Dr. Martin Luther King Jr.'s address.*

DR. MARTIN LUTHER KING JR. *being interviewed inside the Lincoln Memorial on the occasion of his "I Have a Dream" speech.*

The next year Congress passed the Civil Rights Act of 1964, making racial discrimination in public places illegal and encouraging equal educational and employment opportunities. Also in 1964, Dr. King was awarded the Nobel Peace Prize. The great civil rights leader was struck down by an assassin's bullet on April 4, 1968, but he had lived to see a beginning made on his dream.

Martin Luther King Jr. was born on January 15, 1929. In 1983 an act of Congress made Dr. King's birthday a federal holiday to be observed each year on the third Monday of January. Every year since 1991 the National Park Service, in partnership with the Washington, D.C., school system, has held a commemorative birthday ceremony for Dr. King at the Lincoln Memorial.

On January 14, 2000, the first birthday observance of the new millennium was held at the Lincoln Memorial for Dr. King. The large audience included hundreds of Washington, D.C., school students. They listened to the recorded voice of Dr. King delivering his "I Have a Dream" speech at the very spot where they were standing. In his keynote address, Michael L. Ferrell, Executive Director of the Coalition for the Homeless, noted that "I Have a Dream" had been chosen as the most important political speech of the twentieth century in a research survey of university professors of political science.

At the birthday ceremony that January day, Michael Weaver, a student at Rudolph Elementary School in Washington, told the audience how he had re-enacted Dr. King's "I Have Dream" speech in a school program that had been put on at the Lincoln Memorial. "The first time I read his speech, it taught me something," Michael said. "It taught me to love and not hate."

What better place than the Lincoln Memorial for those words to have been spoken!

THE WREATH PRESENTATION *at the Dr. Martin Luther King Jr. birthday ceremony on January 14, 2000.*

CHAPTER SEVEN

The Lincoln Legacy

THROUGHOUT MUCH OF ITS HISTORY, the ground-level area of the Lincoln Memorial was nothing but a basement containing restrooms and an elevator to take handicapped visitors to the main memorial chamber. But in 1994, 560 square feet (52 square meters) of the space between the restrooms and the elevator was transformed into an exhibit area, a minimuseum, where visitors can learn about the history of the memorial, the wisdom and courage of the man who inspired it, and how the Lincoln Memorial has become the focal point for Americans seeking or expressing their civil rights.

The story of the transformation began in 1989 when a few students from Saguaro High School in Scottsdale, Arizona, visited the great Washington landmark.

The Scottsdale group, twelve in number, had come to Washington with their history teacher, John Calvin, to take part in a week-long program sponsored by the Close Up Foundation. The purpose of the program is to make student visits to the nation's capital more than sightseeing trips, to give students a "close-up" look at the way their government works. The goal of the foundation is to motivate young people to become actively involved in the world around them.

On their free day from the Close Up program, Calvin and his students did their sightseeing and ended up at the Lincoln Memorial. After they looked at Lincoln's statue and his great speeches, the students wanted to know where Dr. King had stood when he made his "I Have a Dream" speech. Calvin showed them where the great civil rights leader had stood, and then the students wanted to know why there was no plaque to mark the spot. There should be one, they said.

They returned to Scottsdale, but some of the group wouldn't let go of the idea of a plaque for Dr. King at the Lincoln Memorial. Perhaps they were motivated by the fact that at the time Arizona had not yet elected not to observe the Martin Luther King, Jr., birthday federal holiday. Perhaps they remembered the Close Up Foundation's message to get "involved." Their idea was that a copper plaque would be cast from Lincoln pennies contributed by schoolchildren across the nation.

THE LIVELY CENTER *of the ground-level exhibits is a mini-theater featuring photographs and film clips of national citizen protests and ceremonies for which the Lincoln Memorial has provided a symbolic setting. One of the events shown is the civil rights rally of 1963 which concluded with Dr. Martin Luther King Jr.'s "I Have a Dream" speech.*

Their teacher, John Calvin, told the students he would help, but the main effort would have to be theirs. As it developed, the six girls in the group really pushed the idea—Liz Cohen, Carol Bien-Willner, Jaime Lewis, Carol Mack, Ailene Mass, and Heidi Sherman. First they wrote a petition calling for the plaque. Next they got signatures on the petition, collecting three thousand in the Scottsdale area. During the summer, the "Scottsdale Six," as they came to be known, earned money for a trip back to Washington.

In the fall they returned to the nation's capital to push their idea for a plaque with the Arizona senators and representatives and with other Congressmen who might have a special interest. At first the idea was warmly received, but then someone pointed out that the federal Commemorative Works Act prohibits putting new memorials on already-existing national memorials. Adding a Martin Luther King Jr. memorial plaque to the Lincoln Memorial would be against the law.

What to do? The students learned that the National Park Service was planning to improve the ground-level visitors' area of the Lincoln Memorial as part of a major rehabilitation project. The students met with Park officials and proposed that part of the improvement could be exhibits telling the history of the memorial and its importance to America. The Park staff liked what they heard and asked the students for more specifics about the exhibits.

Six weeks later, the Scottsdale Six were back in Washington—with travel help from local citizens—and made their presentation to the Park Service. The students said that if the exhibits were approved, they wanted to help design them. The Park Service agreed but wanted students' ideas from all parts of the country.

In a selection campaign put on with the help of the American Federation of Teachers and the Close Up Foundation, seventeen high school students from across the country were brought to the National Park Service's Interpretive Design Center in Harpers Ferry, West Virginia. In an intense four-day session, the professional staff of the center listened to the students' ideas, discussed them, and began to work on the technical details of turning the Lincoln Memorial basement into a visitors' center exhibit area. They all agreed that the exhibits should be called "The Lincoln Legacy."

Meanwhile, the idea of contributions of pennies from school-children to help pay for the project had not been forgotten. A fund-raising campaign called "Pennies Make a Monumental Difference" raised more than sixty thousand dollars.

The Lincoln Memorial exhibit area was dedicated and opened to the public on September 23, 1994. It was truly a statement of Lincoln's legacy. The walls are decorated with twelve black marble tablets bearing some of Lincoln's memorable words. One exhibit tells the story of building the memorial. A video room and gallery tells of important events that have taken place at the Memorial.

Of the original Scottsdale Six, four were able to return to Washington for the dedication. And John Calvin was there, proud of what his students, the first group and those who had followed them, had accomplished for their country.

IN THE EXHIBIT AREA, *school students read some of Abraham Lincoln's famous words carved on massive tablets of black Tennessee marble.*

AFTERWORD

Preserving the Lincoln Memorial

ON A COOL SPRING EVENING in 1929, Daniel Chester French, then seventy-nine years old, returned to the Lincoln Memorial for what he knew would probably be the last time. With him was his daughter Margaret French Cresson. They paused at the foot of the steps to look up at the glorious white temple and at the seated figure of Abraham Lincoln.

After a few moments French turned to his daughter. "Margaret," he said, "I'd like to see what this will look like a thousand years from now."

As he stood before the Lincoln Memorial that night, perhaps French was thinking about the ruins of the Parthenon in Greece. Perhaps he was thinking of the Roman Colosseum or the remains of Stonehenge in England. He knew that monuments, even those built of stone, are at the mercy of time and history.

As a new century and a new millennium begin, the Lincoln Memorial is structurally sound, but it is undergoing extensive rehabilitation, which includes repair, cleaning, and mural restoration. The rehabilitation began in 1991 and is scheduled for completion in 2003. According to Stephen Lorenzetti, Chief of Resource Management for National Park Central, National Park Service, the cost of the memorial's rehabilitation probably will be between $16 and $17 million.

THE CLEANING AND WAXING *of the white marble interior ceiling panels is crucial to the transmission of natural light into the memorial chambers.*

The entire roof of the memorial has been repaired. The center roof, called a "greenhouse roof," has glass panels that transmit natural light to the interior ceiling panels, which are made of white Alabama marble. The greenhouse glass panels were cleaned and replaced as necessary, and the frames were cleaned, repainted, and reinstalled. The marble ceiling panels were cleaned and waxed to better transmit light from the skylight.

The frieze above the colonnade was cleaned, and all marble slabs around the memorial were repointed—that is, crumbling mortar was removed and replaced with fresh mortar. Fortunately, no stone replacement on the memorial has been necessary thus far.

A low-voltage deterrent system was installed to try to keep out birds who find the Lincoln Memorial a comfortable resting or nesting place. At the present time, the Park Service has not been able to find an acceptable method to discourage birds from perching on Lincoln's shoulders!

The walkway leading to the memorial, known as the approach way, has been replaced. As many of the original river stones as could be salvaged were used in the replacement.

The statue of Lincoln will be thoroughly cleaned, but otherwise it is in excellent condition.

The most complex and time-consuming part of the rehabilitation project has been the restoration of the two large symbolic murals mounted high on the north and south walls of the memorial. These murals were painted by Jules Guérin, a 19th century artist noted for his murals in many public buildings in the United States.

The main theme of the mural on the south wall is freedom. The central panel of this mural shows the Angel of Truth giving freedom to a slave and symbolizes Lincoln's emancipation of the American slaves. In the central panel of the mural on the north wall, the Angel of Truth joins the hands of figures representing the North and South, symbolizing Lincoln's triumph in preserving the Union.

The color and vibrancy of the original paintings was almost hidden by decades of accumulated dirt, smoke, and other grime. Because of the severe fluctuation between summer heat and winter cold, the murals' paint was cracked and flaked in many places. The work of cleaning the murals and stabilizing the cracking and flaking was highly technical. The leader of the team conserving the murals, Christiana Cunningham-Adams, was trained in Rome and had helped to restore wall paintings in the Basilica of St. Francis of Assisi. The conservation work on the Lincoln Memorial murals began in 1995 and was completed in 1996. Plans are now being developed for long-term protection of these murals.

INFORMATION
About the Lincoln Memorial

THE LINCOLN MEMORIAL is open to the public from 8:00 A.M. until 11:45 P.M., every day except Christmas Day. There is no admission charge.

MEMORIAL WEB SITE ADDRESS:
www.nps.gov/linc

THOSE INTERESTED IN LEARNING more about the Lincoln Memorial should contact the National Park Service as specified below:

Address: National Capital Parks–Central
The National Mall
900 Ohio Drive, S.W.
Washington, D.C. 20242

Telephone: (202) 426–6841

BIBLIOGRAPHY

Angle, Paul M., ed. *The Lincoln Reader.* New York: Da Capo Press, 1990. (Originally published, Westport, CT: Greenwood Press, 1947.)

Ashabranner, Brent. *A Memorial for Mr. Lincoln.* New York: G.P. Putnam's Sons, 1992.

_____. *The New African Americans.* North Haven, CT: Linnet Books, 1999.

Biel, Timothy Levi. *The Civil War.* San Diego: Lucent Books, 1991.

Burchard, Hank. "Making Their Mark at the Memorial." *The Washington Post*, November 18, 1994.

Cresson, Margaret French. *Journey into Fame: The Life of Daniel Chester French.* Cambridge, MA: Harvard University Press, 1947.

Freedman, Russell. *Lincoln: A Photobiography.* New York: Clarion Books, 1987.

Fry, Smith D. *Patriotic Story of the Lincoln Memorial.* Washington, DC: Model Printing Company, 1923.

Levine, Susan. "A Capital Celebration: Huge Crowd Revels in Festival of Light, Sound." *The Washington Post*, January 1, 2000.

Lincoln Memorial. Washington, DC: Division of Publications, National Park Service, 1986. (Official National Park Handbook, No. 29).

McPherson, James M. *Abraham Lincoln and the Second American Revolution*. New York: Oxford University Press, 1990.

Richmond, Michael. "Building Lincoln's Memorial." *The Washington Post*, February 13, 1984.

Rosenfeld, Megan, and Teresa Wittz. "Performance: on the Mall and Beyond, a Night of Epoch, and Odd, Proportions. *The Washington Post*, January 1, 2000.

Sandburg, Carl. *Abraham Lincoln: The War Years*, Vol. 4. New York: Harcourt Brace and World, 1939.

Sefton, Dru. "'I Have a Dream': In a Century of a Speeches, Certain Words Still Soar." *USA Today*, December 30, 1999.

Trescott, Jacqueline. "Marian Anderson's Voice of Conscience." *The Washington Post*, May 3, 1991.

Washington, James Melvin, ed. *A Monument of Hope: The Essential Writings of Martin Luther King Jr.* San Francisco: Harper & Row, 1986.

INDEX

Page numbers in *italics* refer to illustrations.